Looking at . . .
New Dinosaur Discoveries

THE NEW
DINOSAUR
COLLECTION

For a free color catalog describing Gareth Stevens' list of high-quality books and multimedia programs, call 1-800-542-2595 (USA) or 1-800-461-9120 (Canada). Gareth Stevens Publishing's Fax: (414) 225-0377. See our catalog, too, on the World Wide Web: http://gsinc.com

Library of Congress Cataloging-in-Publication Data

Green, Tamara, 1945-
    Looking at-- new dinosaur discoveries/by Tamara Green;
illustrated by Tony Gibbons. -- North American ed.
      p. cm. -- (The new dinosaur collection)
    Includes index.
    Summary: Describes the most recent discoveries about how the
dinosaurs lived and how they became extinct.
    ISBN 0-8368-1792-3 (lib. bdg.)
    1. Dinosaurs--Juvenile literature. [1. Dinosaurs.] I. Gibbons,
Tony, ill. II. Title. III. Series.
QE862.D5G7347   1997
567.9--dc21   97-554

This North American edition first published in 1997 by
Gareth Stevens Publishing
1555 North RiverCenter Drive, Suite 201
Milwaukee, Wisconsin 53212 USA

This U.S. edition © 1997 by Gareth Stevens, Inc. Created with original © 1996
by Quartz Editorial Services, 112 Station Road, Edgware HA8 7AQ U.K.

Consultant: Dr. David Norman, director of the Sedgwick Museum of Geology,
University of Cambridge, England.

Additional artwork by Clare Heronneau.

Printed in the United States of America

1 2 3 4 5 6 7 8 9 01 00 99 98 97

Looking at . . .
New Dinosaur Discoveries

by Tamara Green

Illustrated by Tony Gibbons

Gareth Stevens Publishing
MILWAUKEE

Contents

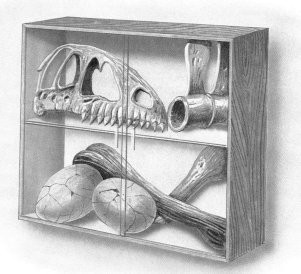

Introduction

A new type of dinosaur has been discovered every two months or so over the last few years. In fact, over 350 different species have been unearthed so far.

Scientists are also continually finding out more about these fascinating prehistoric creatures. As a result, there are many intriguing new theories about the way dinosaurs lived, as well as why they became extinct 65 million years ago.

How much do you know about dinosaurs?

As you turn the pages that follow, you'll discover how new types are named; come face-to-face with some recent, exciting finds; and learn about new ideas concerning dinosaur extinction. You'll also be able to take a look inside an 80-million-year-old dinosaur egg that never hatched.

So join our exciting journey of discovery. Many amazing new facts are about to unfold for you. Soon, you'll be up-to-date with all sorts of dinosaur data.

5

Rare find

Lin Spearpoint's hobby is certainly an exciting one! She had just become interested in fossil-hunting when, by an amazing piece of good luck, she discovered an almost complete skeleton of a **Polacanthus** (POLE-A-CAN-THUS) near her home. It is one of the world's rarest dinosaurs and has a name meaning "many spines."

This armored dinosaur was an herbivore that lived about 115 million years ago in Early Cretaceous times. The skeleton Lin discovered on the Isle of Wight off the southern coast of England was probably that of a fully grown **Polacanthus**. It measured 12 feet (3.6 meters) in length and 5 feet (1.5 m) in height.

First, Lin had obtained the permission of a local farmer to dig on his land. Before long, she found thousands of fragments of fossilized bone, which another collector helped identify. "We can tell from the geology of the area," Lin explains, "that in Cretaceous times there was a river here. It is possible that many dinosaurs may have drowned in it, including my **Polacanthus**."

The **Polacanthus** has not yet been completely restored, but it is already on display at a theme park on the Isle of Wight. Although it must be very valuable, Lin does not want to sell the skeleton. She prefers that her dinosaur remain on the island.

With an ambition to discover a completely new type of dinosaur, Lin hopes to join a dig.

She would love to go on a fossil-hunting expedition somewhere exotic like the Gobi Desert in Mongolia. Since she struck so lucky once, the experts would probably be pleased to have this amateur fossil hunter join them in digging for other dinosaur remains!

7

Antarctic

When today's explorers visit Antarctica in the remote Southern Hemisphere, what they find is an enormous, empty landscape. For the most part, the environment is just ice or bare rock, and there is very little plant or animal life. Conditions are harsh, and temperatures reach as low as -76° Fahrenheit (-60° Centigrade).

But Antarctica was not always a frozen continent. The climate there during Jurassic and Cretaceous times was probably much milder than it is today. Millions of years ago, there would have been abundant animal life, as well as thick forests, in the area we now call Antarctica.

Antarctica was once part of the supercontinent of Gondwana. This included South America, India, Africa, and Australia, too, before they broke away and separated. Dinosaurs have been found on all these landmasses.

So it is perhaps not surprising that paleontologists have recently found dinosaur bones on Antarctica. The first of these was a Cretaceous

dinosaurs

Another discovery, made by Dr. J. J. Hooker while on an expedition with the British Antarctic Survey, was a Cretaceous ornithopod that seems to be related to **Hypsilophodon** (HIP-SEE-LOAF-OH-DON). Neither of these dinosaurs has been given a name yet.

A third interesting and much older find dates from Early Jurassic times and has been named **Cryolophosaurus ellioti** (CRY-OL-OFF-OH-SAW-RUS ELL-EE-OH-TEE), which means "Elliot's frozen crested reptile." As you can tell from its name, this carnivore probably had a crest on its head that looked like the one on the dinosaur **Dilophosaurus** (DIE-LOAF-OH-SAW-RUS).

Experts are optimistic that more discoveries of dinosaur remains will eventually be made in Antarctica. Maybe there will even be some excitingly different species.

ankylosaur that lived about 80 million years ago. Its remains were found on James Ross Island by a group of Argentinian geologists.

9

look inside

American paleontologists were very excited in 1995. In Argentina, the fossilized egg of a rare, long-necked, armored herbivore from Cretaceous times was discovered. An adult **Saltasaurus** (SAL-TA-SAW-RUS), they knew, was 40 feet (12 m) long, with bony plates and studs on its back for protection against threatening predators. But no one knew what **Saltasaurus** young looked like.

The newly discovered egg was about half the size of a football, about 70 million years old, and in very good condition. Such perfect fossilized dinosaur eggs are rare. Perhaps it had not hatched because the mother was attacked and had to abandon it.

Experts in Miami, Florida, did not want to destroy the egg in order to look inside, of course. So they decided to use a scanner to view the contents.

10

an egg!

The scan gave them a sort of X-ray picture. Sure enough, it revealed a tiny baby dinosaur; but it was at a very early stage of development. Its bones had not even formed properly yet. The scientists were disappointed but still hope to find another perfect **Saltasaurus** egg, this time with a fully developed baby inside that would have been just about ready to hatch.

In the Gobi Desert of Mongolia, meanwhile, scientists discovered the first embryo of a dinosaur they think would have grown up to be an **Oviraptor** (OVE-EE-RAP-TOR). This time, they did not need to scan the egg to see inside it. Half of the egg had been worn away, and the almost fully developed baby was visible. About 80 million years ago, it probably looked just like the illustration shown here, with its head tucked up against its knees, and its tail curled around the inside of the egg.

In the past, dinosaurs were often named after the person who sponsored an expedition or made the discovery. For example, **Baryonyx walkeri** (<u>BAR</u>-EE-<u>ON</u>-ICKS <u>WALK</u>-ER-EE) was found by the British amateur fossil hunter William Walker, and its name means "Walker's heavy-claw."

Recently, several paleontologists have been more imaginative. For instance, one pterodactyl was named after Sir Arthur Conan Doyle, 19th-century author of *The Lost World*, a novel about a land where dinosaurs survived.

The new pterodactyl, found in Brazil and with a wingspan of 20 feet (6 m), has been named **Arthurdactylus conan-doylei** (<u>ARTHUR</u>-DAK-<u>TEE</u>-LOOS <u>COE</u>-NAN-<u>DOY</u>-LAY). Shown *above*, it is now in the state Natural History Museum in Karlsruhe, Germany.

Sometimes new dinosaurs are named after companies that donate money toward a dinosaur dig. **Atlascopcosaurus** (<u>AT</u>-LAS-<u>COP</u>-CO-<u>SAW</u>-RUS), *right*, for instance, is named after the Australian mining company that contributed toward its discovery.

discoveries

Steven Spielberg, director of the movie *Jurassic Park*, recently sponsored a dig in China. One of the finds was a Jurassic ankylosaur. They named it **Tianchiasaurus** (TEE-AN-KEE-A-SAW-RUS), which means "heavenly lizard." But they also gave it a second name, **nedegoapeferima** (NED-EGG-OH-AP-UH-FERRY-MAH), so its full title is **Tianchiasaurus nedegoapeferima**. This second name has no meaning, but is made up of letters from the surnames of the movie's stars — Sam Neill, Laura Dern, Jeff Goldblum, Richard Attenborough, Bob Peck, Martin Ferero, Ariana Richards, and Joseph Mazello.

But one of the strangest dinosaur names of all must be **Irritator** (IRR-IT-ATE-OR). The story behind this name, given to an Early Cretaceous theropod from Brazil, is a curious one. Fossil dealers in Brazil often carve remains into more interesting shapes simply to get more money for them. One was carved to look as if it came from a pterosaur, but experts later found out what had been done and realized that it was in fact from a new type of theropod. They were so angry at what the dealers had done to the remains that they gave the new dinosaur the name **Irritator**, which means "annoying!"

Dino-bird

Is it a bird? Is it a dinosaur? No, it's a dino-bird! Dr. Mark Norell of the American Museum of Natural History has come up with a super new discovery following an expedition to the Gobi Desert in Mongolia.

During a dig lasting ten days, he and his fellow paleontologists found about one hundred Cretaceous dinosaur fossils, twenty-eight eggs, and the remains of two strange creatures, half-bird and half-dinosaur, in the sands at Ukhaa Tolgod. They believe these creatures were unable to fly and evolved many millions of years after **Archaeopteryx** (ARK-EE-OP-TER-ICKS). (**Archaeopteryx** was a birdlike reptile with feathers that scientists think may have been able to fly short distances.)

This dino-bird, which has been named **Mononykus** (MON-OH-NYE-KUS), meaning "one claw," had stubs instead of wings. Scientists now wonder whether the power of flight was perhaps first developed back in prehistoric times, only to be lost and then evolve again. Most scientists would now agree that birds are the distant relatives of dinosaurs.

A dinosaur named Sue

Strange but true — the remains of a magnificent **Tyrannosaurus rex** (TIE-<u>RAN</u>-OH-<u>SAW</u>-RUS <u>RECKS</u>), named Sue by those who found her, cannot be put on exhibit. For the time being, the remains must be kept locked in a large container.

The story of Sue is an extraordinary one. The skeleton was discovered in South Dakota on land leased by the government from a member of the Sioux Indian tribe. The Black Hills Institute of Geological Research then spent two years preparing the specimen for display.

However, in May 1992, federal agents raided the Institute and seized Sue. It was ruled that permission should have been sought from the Secretary of the Interior before the dig was even started since it was on government land.

Sue's skeletal remains are still stuck in that metal container and will have to stay there until the authorities receive an acceptable price for her on behalf of the Sioux. You can see a reconstruction here of what she may have looked like when alive all those millions of years ago. Watch the newspapers for further developments!

Other superb **Tyrannosaurus rex** specimens that the Black Hills Institute has helped to restore and place on exhibit include dinosaurs that have been nicknamed Stan, Duffy, Steven, and County rex. Stan is a particularly well-traveled dinosaur skeleton that has even been to Japan for a **Tyrannosaurus rex** World Exposition. It is probably the largest, most complete **Tyrannosaurus rex** skeleton on display anywhere in the world.

New ideas

Using their computers, a group of scientists came up with an idea about why dinosaurs died out 65 million years ago.

They believe that a large asteroid crashed to Earth at a place called Chiczulub in Mexico, where it made an enormous crater about 180 miles (290 kilometers) wide under the sea. Scientists once thought it was the dust and dirt thrown up by the asteroid that caused the dinosaurs to perish. But now we know differently.

The area where the asteroid crashed is very rich in a substance called sulfur. Because of the asteroid's impact on landing, large amounts

18

on extinction

of this sulfur were forced into the air, creating a haze of mist that blocked all sunlight for about thirty years.

As a result, the temperature fell, and many plants could not survive. This meant that the herbivores starved to death. The carnivorous dinosaurs then had no herbivores on which to prey. Other scientists think that large amounts of a rare substance called selenium may have been released when many volcanoes erupted. Selenium can be very poisonous and may have made the herbivores ill when they ate vegetation that was covered in it. Experts have even found traces of selenium in dinosaur eggs.

Dinosaur update

Here is exciting news straight from the files of some of the most eminent scientists in the field of paleontology.

Another amazing T. rex

Canada is proud of a tremendously exciting recent dinosaur find. **Tyrannosaurus rex** is probably the most famous of all the dinosaurs. Yet only about a dozen or so nearly complete skeletons of this creature have been discovered so far. Now, however, paleontologists have unearthed another that is about 18 feet (5.5 m) high and 49 feet (15 m) long, with enormous teeth. It was discovered in 1994 in the Canadian province of Saskatchewan, near the town of Eastend. A paleontologist who helped with excavating the skeleton reports finding its bones scattered along the side of a river. Since then, he and his team have been successfully piecing it together, bit by bit.

Stolen footprint

Strange but true — a 120-million-year-old dinosaur footprint has disappeared from the Isle of Wight, off the southern coast of England. It was an 18-inch (46-centimeter) **Iguanodon** (IG-WA-NO-DON) track, and scientists believe it must have been cut out of the rock by thieves. The best of three such prints discovered in 1987, it was visible only when the tide was out. Now, sadly, no one will be able to see this interesting dinosaur trace fossil because of the robbery.

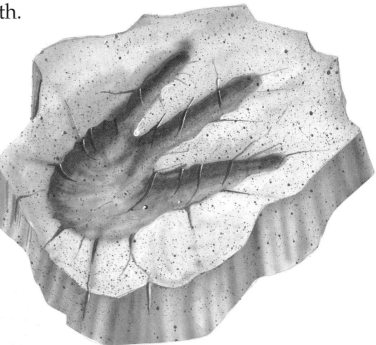

High prices

Dinosaur bones and eggs are now being bought for very high prices, particularly in the United States and Japan. Private dealers and fossil shops are offering them for sale. And sometimes they come up for auction. One American catalog lists fossil specimens priced at more than $150,000; and one wealthy collector paid $500,000 for a skeleton that was still in the ground. Paleontologists are concerned that important sites may be raided for the money that the remains can bring. That is why some countries have decided to ban export of fossils so they can at least stay in the part of the world where they were found. To meet the demands for fossils, some companies are now even making replicas.

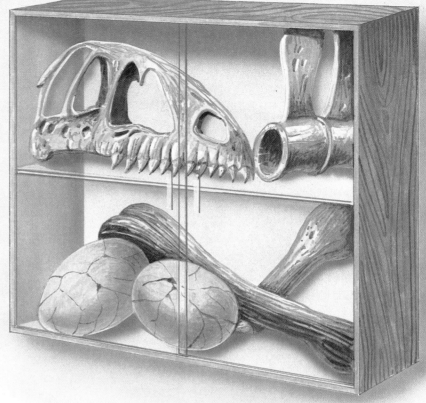

Larger females

Some experts think the females of some types of dinosaurs may have been larger than the males. Among today's reptiles, the females are usually larger and more robust. But so far, the only detailed research in this area has been done on **Tyrannosaurus rex** remains. We will have to wait and see if it was true for all the dinosaurs.

21

More dinosaur news

What else is new in the world of dinosaurs? Keep reading and find out.

Scottish finds

Although there have been many dinosaur discoveries in Great Britain, most of these have been in the south. In fact, until 1995, only a single, fossilized dinosaur footprint, and no bones at all, had been found as far north as Scotland. But the fact that a footprint existed meant bones might be discovered some day, so paleontologists did not give up. Now, on the Isle of Skye, off the coast of Scotland, the skeletal remains of both a sauropod and a theropod have been found. It seems this part of the world must have been home to both herbivores and carnivores. This must have been when the Isle of Skye was still joined to the mainland, because dinosaurs could never have crossed the seas.

Massive find

In the picture *below*, you can see an illustration of a recently unearthed **Giganotosaurus** (JEYE-GAN-OH-TOH SAW-RUS). This late Cretaceous theropod was discovered in Argentina. Experts think it was about 40 feet (12 m) long and that it weighed about 8 tons when alive. The picture shows the bones that were unearthed, in position, and also an outline to give an idea of what this dinosaur looked like when it stalked its victims 70 million years ago.

The hunt for DNA

Experts hope they can find some dinosaur DNA. This is microscopic genetic material that might enable scientists to recreate dinosaurs, just as in the movie *Jurassic Park*. But some scientists say DNA cannot survive more than 100,000 years unless preserved in amber. Dinosaurs died out 65 million years ago. So it may never be possible to recreate them.

Missing link

A wonderful new find was made during 1996 near the city of Madrid in Spain. It was the fossil of a bird that lived about 125 million years ago, so perfect even the feathers and stomach contents are visible. The bird was named **Eoalulavis** (YOH-AH-LOO-LAH-VIS) after the flap, or alula, on each wing that helped the bird control its flight. This is the earliest bird that has been found with such a flap and may be a "missing link" in the evolution of birds from dinosaurs.

Huge skull

Paleontologists have recently announced the discovery in Morocco, North Africa, of a 5-foot (1.5-m)-long skull of what must have been another enormous Cretaceous carnivore. You can see how much bigger it is than a human skull, *above*. Experts believe it belonged to a **Carcharodontosaurus** (CAR-CAR-OH-DONT-OH-SAW-RUS). A complete skeleton of this dinosaur has not yet been found. What a gigantic creature it must have been!

23

GLOSSARY

carnivores — meat-eating animals.

dig (n) — an excavation site where fossils are unearthed.

evolve — to change shape or develop gradually over a long period of time.

expedition — a journey or voyage.

extinct — no longer alive.

fossils — traces or remains of plants and animals found in rock.

herbivores — plant-eating animals.

paleontologists — scientists who study the remains of plants and animals that lived long ago.

predators — animals that kill other animals for food.

remains — a skeleton, bones, or dead body.

sauropods — gigantic, plant-eating dinosaurs with strong legs, long necks, and small heads.

species — a group of animals or plants that are closely related and often very similar in behavior and appearance.

theropods — meat-eating dinosaurs that walked on their hind legs. **Irritator** was an Early Cretaceous theropod from Brazil.

INDEX